Presented to:

---

By:

---

---

---

Date:

---

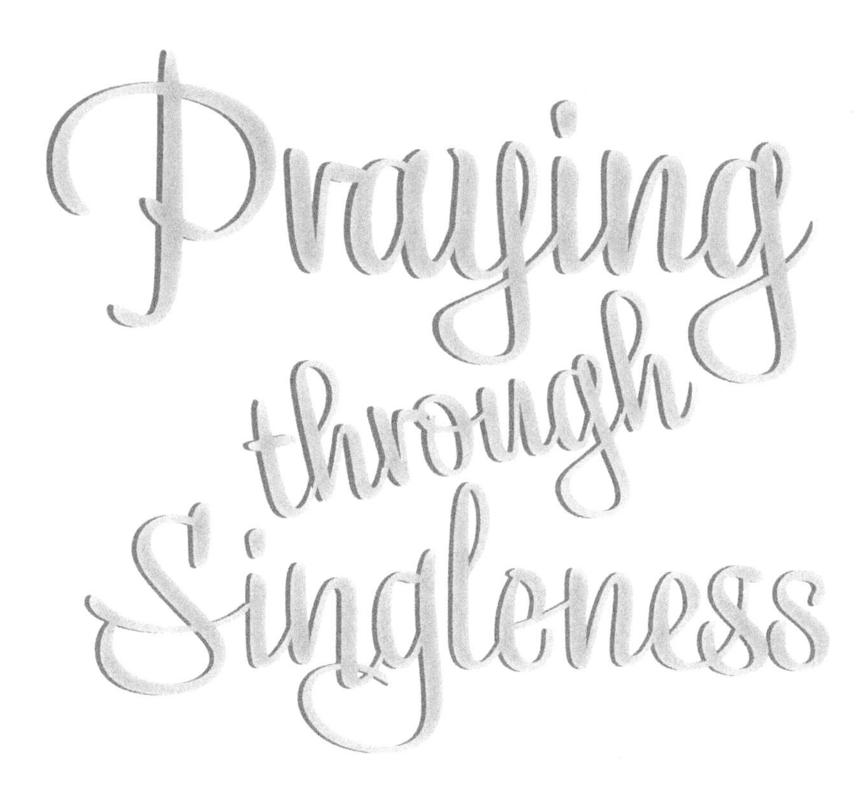


A Guided Prayer Journal for Young Women

Shayla Ortiz

Three Keys Publishing
*Books to Live By*

Published by Three Keys Ministries
Temecula, California, U.S.A.
www.threekeysministries.com
Printed in the U.S.A.


ISBN 978-0-9986000-3-1



Book cover and interior desiign by Designer Girl Graphics

*To My Single Purpose followers.*

*You inspire me.*

"When authors write books geared toward people who are single, it's easy to fall into the trap of getting the audience to focus only on their marital status. Shayla directs the single readers to the first and most important place: their relationship with God."

*Joshua Rogers*
*Columnist at Fox News Opinion*
*Joshuarogers.com*

"*Praying Through Singleness* is an invaluable prayer journal that guides Christian single women to fix their eyes on their Eternal Prince, Jesus Christ. This relationship resource inclines your spiritual ears to hear the heart of the Father while encouraging you to share your heart's desires with the Father. You will be emboldened to both practically and prophetically pen down, pray into, prepare for, and proclaim God's promises over every single step of your life!"

*Elena & Natalia Maranian*
*TV Hosts & Producers, The Elena & Natalia Show*

"*Praying Through Singleness* is a great devotion to get in the habit of journaling, another source to speak to and hear from God. It's a great resource that doesn't last a week, a month, but the accountability is 70 days! By then, many habits, good habits have been formed. I would highly recommend this for teens to adults. A great tool for small groups, conferences, church events, home studies, and more! Thank you Shayla for being obedient to God's calling on starting up a devotion like this."

*Linda Medina*
*Director of Be Mine Conference*
*Bemineconference.org*

"We are excited about the message conveyed in this book! God has given Shayla a heavenly perspective on singleness and we believe it's a message all singles need to read. Shayla's heart for people can be sensed through her writing and we are sure all who read *Praying Through Singleness* will be both highly encouraged and challenged."

*Rolando & Olivia Gonzales*
*Lead Pastors at Reveal Church, Lawrenceville Georgia*
*Revealchurch.org*

"By his own divine hand, God created us individually and specifically for his glory. Every detail was taken into account when creating each of us. *Praying Through Singleness* will help you find the uniqueness as a single woman given to this earth as a gift directly from God. Overwhelmingly, your singleness will be enhanced by allowing your Creator to be the center of your life. Page after page you will be led into a deeper walk with our God."

*Chapelain Karla C. Rossi - Gonzalez*
*Women's Ministry Leader Coral Park Baptist Church*

I would like to express my love and gratitude to my loudest cheerleader of all, my husband, Caesar. Thank you for patiently encouraging me through the dark days and pushing me past my self-imposed limits. This book is truly our labor of love.

Special thanks to Denise Harmer for her keen editing, and thank you to Dee Flores for his stunning photography.

My most sincere gratitude to a feisty woman of God who believed in me, Lynn Donovan. Thank you for seeing my work through the eyes of Christ and fearlessly taking on this project.

I'm genuinely thankful to the talented Dineen Miller. You not only gave my vision color, you brought it to life.

# Contents

# Introduction

They say perspective is everything. The way we view the season we're in directly impacts our attitude and approach. As humans, our field of vision is tied to what we can see with our earthly eyes which is attached to the flesh. But as believers, the Holy Spirit beckons us unto a higher level where the panorama is unobstructed and provides a wider view of where we stand.

Ahhh...the advantage of viewing with our spiritual eyes. A bleak and hopeless outlook visually shifts into an opportunity of growth and greater understanding because of our supernatural visual acuity. As I typed each word in this journal, the Holy Spirit reminded me of the need to emphasize the importance of a holy perspective. So many near-sighted singles are drowning in temporary sorrows which will eventually vanish and be no more. Yet, their obstructed view has bound them to worthlessness, loneliness, and desperation. Wandering aimlessly through an arid desert having lost sight to whom they belong.

God's intention was for his creation to live in paradise and not a fallen world, but the choices made by Adam and Eve in the Garden of Eden determined their future as well as the generations to follow. God's purpose for singleness is that you enjoy an unhampered relentless pursuit of him. Not to live in fear and doubt, plagued with insecurities while making ungodly decisions that will most certainly affect your future and generations to come. From a human perspective, you are single. Alone. One. But in the spirit, you have a plus one. Since before you were born God was already engaged in your life, keeping a watchful eye over you, always by your side making sure to stamp his creation, ***"Fearfully and Wonderfully Made."*** It was in that divine process your journey began.

Years later, the seasons have changed but his ever-presence has been a constant. The journey he forged for you many years ago is still on track. The detours, delays, and setbacks have all been accounted for and worked into his master plan. He's still actively involved in your life but now he's asking you for more.

Your single status is prime real estate for Christ. It's an empty space for him to build, plant, and develop. You're not an empty space; however, the season in which you're living is fertile ground for the Lord's blueprint to come to life! God will begin by preparing the ground and making way for the foundation to be laid, a sturdy foundation on which your future will be built. It's an exciting time to dream, plan, and build up.

God has a plan for your life, and all that comes from God is good. Whatever your future holds, you're in the best hands. Whether it's marriage, mission work, school, or career, the Lord will equip you with everything you need to fulfill it. Through the process it's important to prayerfully prepare, move as the Spirit leads, and stay positive. Praying through singleness was created to help you navigate singlehood through ten weeks of soul-searching prayer. This guided journal will lead you through thought-provoking prompts:

❁Devotional
Each day a short devotional is provided to encourage and stir your spirit. It will prepare your mind for prayer.

❁Key Verse
The Word of God will anchor and steady your soul.

❁Prayer Key
The prayer key will cue you to make specific requests when you pray.

❁God spoke to my heart...
This is a place where you write what God speaks into your heart. Keep in mind that God speaks in many ways. He speaks through his Word, wise counsel, nature, dreams, a song, etc. God cannot be boxed in; he will speak to his sheep and his sheep will hear his voice.

❁My thoughts...
A place is reserved for your thoughts. The purpose is for you to practice journaling and make it a lifelong habit. Write out your thoughts, feelings, fears, ideas, and goals. Writing them on paper will organize your thoughts and relieve the clutter that hampers your mind to focus on what is right and true.

Each day you are encouraged to pray over a different subject; however, allow the Holy Spirit to guide you. If you are led to linger on a page and pray over a specific topic for a couple of days before moving forward, obey his leading. You are walking with the Lord at his pace. There are subjects that require intense prayer more than others. God will draw your attention to pressing matters that need to be addressed and dealt with.

I pray you are blessed and favored as you choose to meet with the Lord in his secret place every day. As you walk with the Lord may he place a new song in your heart. May he arm you with strength to endure and make your way perfect. The Lord is your rock and your fortress as you learn to trust and surrender all things. Fear will vanish as you lean and abide in his perfect will. Honor the Lord and he will honor you. Battle on your knees! Fight for your singleness. Don't allow the enemy to plunder the joy out of your season by growing impatience, persistent doubt, and destructive sin. This is your highly regarded time with God as his set-apart child. Wear your singleness like a crown of distinction. This is your shining moment of preparation, as you allow the Lord to lay the groundwork for your future.

# Week One

## Preparation

Prepare your spirit for a supernatural encounter with your heavenly Bridegroom. This journey is an intimate walk between you and Jesus. Each day will encourage the uncovering of that which might hinder your walk with Christ and therefore lay the foundation for your future blessing.

# Day 1

## Prepare My Heart

As your journey begins, genuinely seek deeper intimacy with Jesus. Choose to spend time in his presence above all things. Keep in mind, the more you seek him the more he will manifest his presence in your life. Speak to him honestly and from the heart, exposing your innermost secrets. Secrets which are already known to him, but as your Abba Father, he desires to hear them spoken by you in a demonstration of trust. Entrust him with your fears and insecurities as a daughter speaks to her daddy. Let him listen to the drama in your life. Share your comings and goings. Make him a part of your plans however silly they may seem. He's interested in everything that deals with you. Remember, with prayer the more you pour out, the more of him will be poured in.

## Key Verse

"But if from there you seek the Lord your God, you will find him if you seek him with all your heart and with all your soul." (Deuteronomy 2:29 NIV)

## Prayer Key

- ❁A receptive heart
- ❁Desire to choose him above all things
- ❁Unabashed honesty
- ❁Pour into me, Lord

God spoke to my heart ...

My thoughts ...

# Day 2

## Prepare My Mind

Your mind is a battleground. Prayer is the spiritual weapon required to conquer the battle and take every thought captive. The moment you decided to take this journey the enemy claimed his position in the frontlines of your mind. He will try to discourage and distract you from praying. Such a battle calls for a strong mind...a Christ-like mind. Prayer creates a connection to the Lord where he is allowed to sync, download, store, and delete information to help you not only conquer the battle but win the war.

## Key Verse

"We demolish arguments and every pretension that sets itself up against the knowledge of God, and we take captive every thought to make it obedient to Christ." (2 Corinthians 10:5 NIV)

## Prayer Key

- ❃Help me stay focused
- ❃Take thoughts captive
- ❃Connection to God
- ❃Give me a Christ-like mind

God spoke to my heart ...

My thoughts ...

# Day 3

## Align My Words

Your words have power. During this journey remember to bring your words into agreement with the Lord. Declare his sovereignty over your life. Decree his promises over your situation. Affirm his truths over the lies in your mind. As you align your words, don't just think them, say them out loud! God spoke this world into existence because his words carried supernatural power. Your words do too! Be mindful of the words you speak from this moment on, remembering to always speak life!

## Key Verse

"The tongue can speak words that bring life or death. Those who love to talk must be ready to accept what it brings." (Proverbs 18:21 ERV)

## Prayer Key

- ❁Align my words
- ❁Mindful of what I speak
- ❁God's truths over lies
- ❁Speak life

God spoke to my heart ...

My thoughts ...

# Day 4

## Prepare the Atmosphere

You may pray in your car or in the shower, trusting the Lord is listening to your prayers; however, this journey is different. There's purpose behind it and that is to seek intimacy with the Lord. Make it a date each and every time you reverently approach your Bridegroom's presence. A special time devoted just to him, the lover of your soul. Set apart a place and time for your daily heavenly encounter. A quiet place with little to no distractions. This will not only help you concentrate but also meditate while being still in his holy presence, becoming receptive to his voice.

## Key Verse

"But when you pray, go into your room, close the door and pray to your Father, who is unseen. Then your Father, who sees what is done in secret, will reward you." (Matthew 6:6 NIV)

## Prayer Key

- ❁I want to be deliberate
- ❁Consecrated space
- ❁Intimacy with the Bridegroom
- ❁Receptiveness to his voice

God spoke to my heart ...

My thoughts ...

# Day 5

## Prepare My Attitude

There is an ongoing battle for your attention in the spiritual realm, so you must be deliberate with your prayer time. Make a conscious decision to place this supernatural appointment at the very top of your agenda, schedule, or whatever you use to organize your time. As you prioritize your time with your Bridegroom, you'll notice your attitude align with your decision to pray.

## Key Verse

"But first and most importantly seek (aim at, strive after) His kingdom and His righteousness [His way of doing and being right—the attitude and character of God], and all these things will be given to you also." (Matthew 6:33 AMP)

## Prayer Key

- ❁Be focused
- ❁Help me organize my time
- ❁Deliberate prayer time
- ❁Align my attitude to yours

God spoke to my heart ...

My thoughts ...

# Day 6

## Prepare My Spirit

You've entered this journey with purpose. It's imperative you give your King access to all aspects of your life. Allow him free reign to adjust, remove, reposition, and repair anything in you that he deems necessary for spiritual growth. Your Abba Father is asking you for a malleable spirit to accomplish his purpose as you walk through this journey together.

## Key Verses

"Create in me a clean heart, O God, and renew a right and steadfast spirit within me." (Psalm 51:10 AMP)

"Restore to me the joy of Your salvation and sustain me with a willing spirit." (Psalm 51:12 AMP)

## Prayer Key

❁Help me let go

❁I give you free reign for change

❁Malleable spirit

❁Clean heart

God spoke to my heart …

My thoughts …

# Day 7

## Prepare Me to Receive

God is not a man, that he should lie. When you delight in the Lord and seek his kingdom above all things, he graciously gives you the desires of your heart. With his promise in mind, delight in the Lord daily through prayer, believing that as you sow your seeds of faith God immediately begins to lay the groundwork for you to reap your harvest. Pray in faith because God is working. Prepare to receive in faith.

## Key Verse

"Take delight in the Lord, and he will give you your heart's desires." (Psalm 37:4 NLT)

## Prayer Key

- ❃Delight in the Lord
- ❃Keep his promises in mind
- ❃A receiving heart
- ❃Prepare in faith

God spoke to my heart …

My thoughts …

# Week Two

## Direction

Your requests this week are eternal things which move God's heart, so stay the course and be consistent, for the Holy Spirit will be working deeply in you. He will be unveiling your eyes enabling you to see what the enemy has concealed as well as directing you in ways you never knew before.

# Day 8

## Direct My Path

God's direction in your life is important because as a human your foresight is limited. Your sight is bound to the things of this world, but God sees things that are hidden from you. A future you can only imagine has already been seen by him. You base your decisions on your perception of circumstances, but God's supernatural orientation gives you advantageous insight. Seek his direction. Trust his direction. Obey his direction.

## Key Verse

"Trust in *and* rely confidently on the Lord with all your heart And do not rely on your own insight *or* understanding. In all your ways know *and* acknowledge *and* recognize Him, and He will make your paths straight *and* smooth [removing obstacles that block your way]." (Proverbs 3:5-6 AMP)

## Prayer Key

- ❁Clear direction in my life
- ❁Revelation
- ❁Trust your direction
- ❁Obey your direction

God spoke to my heart ...

My thoughts ...

# Day 9

## Give Me Revelation

Divine revelation walks hand in hand when asking for God's direction. God gives his guidance freely, but you need divine revelation to understand it. Ask your heavenly Father to reveal which way your life should go and how to go about it. As you place your request at his feet, read the Word continually positioning yourself to hear his response. There will be no confusion nor guesswork involved when God's revelation follows direction.

## Key Verse

"Lord, help me learn your ways. Show me how you want me to live." (Psalm 25:4 ERV)

## Prayer Key

- ❀Clear revelation for my life
- ❀Obedience to follow it
- ❀Give me eyes to see and ears to hear

God spoke to my heart …

My thoughts …

# Day 10

## Reroute My Life

When you ask the Lord to take the reins of your life, he'll reveal things which are unknown to you. He will straighten things you didn't know were crooked. Perhaps highlighting a sin that is hindering or blocking a blessing. Allow the Lord to reroute your life and bring it into agreement with his will. This step of obedience will increase your intimacy with your Bridegroom and heighten your ability to hear his voice.

## Key Verse

"If you keep yourself pure, you will be a special utensil for honorable use. Your life will be clean, and you will be ready for the Master to use you for every good work." (2 Timothy 2:21 NLT)

## Prayer Key

❀Take the reins, Lord

❀Reroute my life

❀Highlight the sin in my life

❀Help me be obedient

God spoke to my heart …

My thoughts …

# Day 11

## Sensitivity to the Spirit

Being sensitive to the Spirit's leading is pivotal in your walk with Christ. His guiding hand will lead you, helping to prevent pitfalls that perhaps have shackled you in the past. As the Spirit within you increases, his promptings will be more frequent and notable. His urgings will move you in unexpected directions. He will draw you to love, compassion, and many other things that are honorable and pleasing to your Father.

## Key Verse

"The sinful nature wants to do evil, which is just the opposite of what the Spirit wants. And the Spirit gives us desires that are the opposite of what the sinful nature desires. These two forces are constantly fighting each other, so you are not free to carry out your good intentions. But when you are directed by the Spirit, you are not under obligation to the law of Moses." (Galatians 5:17-18 NLT)

## Prayer Key

- ❁Lead me
- ❁Help me be sensitive to your Spirit
- ❁May you increase as I decrease
- ❁Sensitive to your promptings

God spoke to my heart ...

My thoughts ...

# Day 12

## Give Me a Discerning Heart

The ability to distinguish right from wrong or truths from lies will help keep you from stumbling through your singleness and every other area of your life. Discernment comes from knowing the Word of God and filling yourself with his truth and knowledge. Prayer combined with God's truth gives way to discernment. This is invaluable when choosing between good and God's best.

## Key Verse

"Who is wise? Let them realize these things. Who is discerning? Let them understand. The ways of the Lord are right; the righteous walk in them, but the rebellious stumble in them." (Hosea 14:9 NIV)

## Prayer Key

- ❁Discerning heart
- ❁May I distinguish what is right and wrong
- ❁Know truths from lies
- ❁Help me choose between good and your best

God spoke to my heart …

My thoughts …

# Day 13

## Fill Me with Your Truth

The more you read God's Word the more God's truth will fill and become a part of you. God's truth has the power to render all the lies in your life inert. Lack of spiritual knowledge invites a lie to become true. Filling your mind, heart, and spirit with God's Word empowers you to defeat the lies and embrace God's truth.

## Key Verse

"Finally, believers, whatever is true, whatever is honorable and worthy of respect, whatever is right *and* confirmed by God's Word, whatever is pure and wholesome, whatever is lovely and brings peace, whatever is admirable and of good repute; if there is any excellence, if there is anything worthy of praise, think *continually* on these things [center your mind on them, and implant them in your heart]." (Philippians 4:8 AMP)

## Prayer Key

❁Fill my heart with your truth

❁Give me spiritual knowledge

❁Help me embrace your truth

❁Empower me

God spoke to my heart …

My thoughts …

# Day 14

## Speak into My Heart

When asking for spiritual direction, it's important to take some time to listen. Sit in the stillness of God's presence and let him speak into your heart. Remember your relationship with your Bridegroom is a two-way relationship. As you lay your requests before him, be mindful of his voice. Be still and pay attention. It's in these intimate moments when the lover of your soul will reveal little treasures for you to receive and grow.

## Key Verse

"Ask me and I will tell you remarkable secrets you do not know about things to come." (Jeremiah 33:3 NLT)

## Prayer Key

❁Help me be still

❁Give me ears to hear

❁Speak into my heart

❁Receive and grow

God spoke to my heart …

My thoughts …

# Week Three

## My Identity

What the world has distorted, God wants to reset and bring into alignment with him. Once your system is rebooted and you are synced with your Creator, he will then be free to delete and download. You will no longer grapple with who you think you are but have the security of knowing whose you are.

# Day 15

## My Identity in Christ

You've been walking intimately with your Father for the past three weeks. As your journey progresses, you're becoming vulnerable before the Lord, allowing him to align your life with his will. His alignment will bring into agreement your identity as well. Your Bridegroom will gently help you shed your old natural identity as well as find your new spiritual identity in him. Your transformation has begun, and it looks beautiful.

## Key Verse

"Therefore, if anyone is in Christ, the new creation has come: The old has gone, the new is here!" (2 Corinthians 5:17 NIV)

## Prayer Key

- ❁Align my identity to yours
- ❁Shed my old identity
- ❁Take on Christ's identity
- ❁Help me perceive my transformation

God spoke to my heart …

My thoughts …

# Day 16

## The Mind of Christ

The world says, think positive and create happiness. As a child of God you know that no matter how positive your thoughts, your own strength will never compare to having the mind of Christ. His mind gives you a heavenly perspective to understand his purpose and plans. It provides discernment which sheds light on the dark and makes the wrong clear, for your protection. As his child, he freely gives you this precious gift.

## Key Verse

"Let this mind be in you which was also in Christ Jesus."
(Philippians 2:5 NKJV)

## Prayer Key

❁Put on Christ's mind

❁Give me a heavenly perspective

❁Increase my discernment

God spoke to my heart …

My thoughts …

# Day 17

## THE EYES OF CHRIST

Your self-image is very important to Jesus. He desires that you perceive what he views in you. His hands created you, therefore he's quite proud of you—his creation. When you delight in him but doubt your worth, it grieves his heart. As you take on his identity, he wants you to release the old and embrace the new. Let go of the old perception of yourself and receive the new. You are BEAUTIFUL!

## KEY VERSE

"Because you are precious in My sight, You are honored and I love you." (Isaiah 43:4 AMP)

## PRAYER KEY

❁Renew my self-image

❁Give me eyes to see

❁My worth is in you, Lord

❁Help me embrace my identity

God spoke to my heart …

My thoughts …

# Day 18

## THE HANDS OF CHRIST

You're growing daily in the Lord, step by step progressing through your journey. The relationship with your Bridegroom is deepening naturally, calling you for more. He's calling you to put your faith into practice. The fullness of the Spirit you are experiencing is meant to propel you for his service. Surrender as the Spirit prompts and leads you to serve his people.

## KEY VERSE

"In everything I showed you [by example] that by working hard in this way you must help the weak and remember the words of the Lord Jesus, that He Himself said, 'It is more blessed [and brings greater joy] to give than to receive.'" (Acts 20:35 AMP)

## PRAYER KEY

- ❀Give me a heart to serve
- ❀Reveal the needs of your people
- ❀Receptive to your prompting
- ❀Serve for your glory

God spoke to my heart ...

My thoughts ...

# Day 19

## The Feet of Christ

Having the feet of Christ enables you to walk on water. He's urging you to trust his feet and step out of your boat and venture outside of what feels comfortable. His feet will carry you to places you never thought of pursuing. Your prayer journey with Jesus has strengthened you to take that step of faith. Focus on your Father as you step into your purpose.

## Key Verse

"Even to your old age and gray hairs I am he, I am he who will sustain you. I have made you and I will carry you; I will sustain you and I will rescue you." (Isaiah 46:4 NIV)

## Prayer Key

❁Help me trust you

❁Strengthen me to leave my comfort zone

❁Carry me

❁Focus on Jesus

God spoke to my heart ...

My thoughts ...

# Day 20

## The Reflection of Christ

Your Bridegroom is mesmerized by you. He loves every aspect of your person. He was detailed and intentional when he knit you together. His design was perfect. No flaw can be found in your design. Everything you see within your reflection was deliberate. It grieves him when you fail to see the beauty he sees when he looks at you. Each and every time you enter his presence, allow his Spirit to readjust your self-image and align with his vision.

## Key Verse

"I will give thanks and praise to You, for I am fearfully and wonderfully made; Wonderful are Your works, and my soul knows it very well." (Psalms 139:14 AMP)

## Prayer Key

- Align your self-image with God's vision
- See the beauty that he sees
- May I see Christ's reflection in the mirror
- Help me believe I'm fearfully and wonderfully made

God spoke to my heart ...

My thoughts ...

# Day 21

## THE SPIRIT OF CHRIST

Grant the Holy Spirit full access to your heart, mind, and spirit. Let him do the work to prepare you for the future you desire. He will strengthen, guide, and intercede for you perfectly, in every way. His direction is pivotal in your spiritual growth. The more you allow the Spirit of Christ to increase within you, the louder his voice becomes. His increasing presence will change your perspective, desires, choices, and thoughts. Welcome him.

## KEY VERSE

"In the same way the Spirit [comes to us and] helps us in our weakness. We do not know what prayer to offer or how to offer it as we should, but the Spirit Himself [knows our need and at the right time] intercedes on our behalf with sighs and groanings too deep for words." (Romans 8:26 AMP)

## PRAYER KEY

❈Welcome Holy Spirit

❈I give you control

❈Help me in all ways

❈May I hear your voice

God spoke to my heart …

My thoughts …

# Week Four

## Surrender

God the Father has bestowed you with free will. Voluntary submission allows the Lord to work in and through you. Denying the flesh will unlock blessings that will have far-reaching effects.

# Day 22

## My Will

Your will dictates your actions and plans and leaves you with a false sense of control. Offer up your desire for control to the Lord. His will is perfect. Your will is flawed. Your will is attached to the desires of your flesh and therefore must be surrendered to his Lordship. In order to make wise decisions concerning your future, align your will with his.

## Key Verse

"Teach me to do Your will [so that I may please You], for You are my God; Let Your good Spirit lead me on level ground." (Psalm 143:10 AMP)

## Prayer Key

❁Lord, let your will be my will

❁I surrender my will

❁Take control, Lord

God spoke to my heart …

My thoughts …

# Day 23

## My Life

When you decide to surrender all to the Lord, you cannot compartmentalize submission. It's all or nothing. Yesterday you surrendered your will, today God calls you to surrender your life. It's impossible to honor God and follow his will if you hold a tight grip on your life decisions. Your Father's plans require total surrender so he can work and activate your future blessing. Let go and watch God work.

## Key Verse

"If you fully obey the Lord your God and carefully keep all his commands that I am giving you today, the Lord your God will set you high above all the nations of the world." (Deuteronomy 28:1 NLT)

## Prayer Key

- ❁I surrender my life
- ❁May your will be my will
- ❁I surrender to your plans
- ❁Activate my future blessing

God spoke to my heart ...

My thoughts ...

# Day 24

## Things I Cannot Control

There are many things in life you can control, but as you walk with the Lord, he will allow circumstances to enter into your life for the sole purpose of creating awareness of your need of him. Hardships, illness, death are things that will remind you of God's supremacy. Make it a point not to worry about circumstances you cannot control and surrender them to the Lord. God needs your undivided attention without distraction during this journey.

## Key Verse

"I form the light and create darkness, I bring prosperity and create disaster; I, the Lord, do all these things." (Isaiah 45:7 NIV)

## Prayer Key

- ❁Surrender things I cannot control
- ❁Make me aware of my need for you
- ❁I choose surrender over worry
- ❁Help me give you my undivided attention

God spoke to my heart ...

My thoughts ...

# Day 25

## My Plans

You have many plans for your future. Those plans may include school, a career, marriage, or children. But for those plans to succeed, you must place them before the feet of Jesus. He knows the future, which is hidden from you; therefore, he knows if those plans will be beneficial or destructive for your life. He also knows the best timing in which to make them happen. He sees past your timeline. Entrust your plans to him and watch them come to fruition.

## Key Verse

"Commit your works to the Lord [submit and trust them to Him], and your plans will succeed [if you respond to his will and guidance]." (Proverbs 3:6 AMP)

## Prayer Key

❁I surrender my plans

❁Help me trust you

❁Align my plans with your plans

❁Help me trust your timing

God spoke to my heart …

My thoughts …

# Day 26

## My Dreams

Your dreams are very important to your Father because He, himself, embedded them in your depths. He yearns to be an active partner in every area of your life. He's aware that sometimes your heart dreams of impossible things, far-reaching things, that in your mind will forever stay a "dream." He's reminding you today that you believe in a God in which all things are possible. Share your dreams with him, no matter how crazy they may appear to be. Confidently place them in the dream-givers hands.

## Key Verse

"Now to Him who is able to [carry out His purpose and] do superabundantly more than all that we dare ask or think [infinitely beyond our greatest prayers, hopes, or dreams], according to His power that is at work within us." (Ephesians 3:20 AMP)

## Prayer Key

- ❁I surrender my dreams
- ❁I believe all things are possible
- ❁Be an active partner in my life
- ❁May my dreams bring you glory

God spoke to my heart ...

My thoughts ...

# Day 27

## My Future

When you think of your future, you envision big things. This vision might include falling in love by a certain age. Perhaps career goals that require a disciplined timetable. It's crucial to surrender your future timeline to your Heavenly Father to ensure your vision aligns with his. Your future plans are nearsighted. He knows the future you haven't lived yet. Let his insight influence your steps and choices which ultimately shape your future.

## Key Verse

"My future is in your hands." (Psalm 31:15 NLT)

## Prayer Key

❁I surrender my future

❁Align my vision with yours

❁Influence my steps and choices

God spoke to my heart …

My thoughts …

# Day 28

## My Flesh

Your flesh and the Spirit are in constant conflict with one another. One is led by the sinful nature while the other desires to submit and obey the Lord, but there is good news. You belong to Jesus Christ; therefore, your sinful nature has been crucified. Yes, the struggle is real, but when you walk by the Spirit, sin no longer controls you. This encapsulates the significance of seeking the Lord on a daily basis and clothing yourself with Jesus Christ, to assure you're in step with the Spirit.

## Key Verse

"Let not sin therefore reign in your mortal body, to make you obey its passions. Do not present your members to sin as instruments for unrighteousness, but present yourselves to God as those who have been brought from death to life, and your members to God as instruments for righteousness. For sin will have no dominion over you, since you are not under law but under grace." (Romans 6:12-14 ESV)

## Prayer Key

- ❁Forgive my sins
- ❁I surrender my flesh and sinful desires
- ❁Help me walk by the Spirit and abide in you

God spoke to my heart …

My thoughts …

# Week Five

## Application

It is one thing to read the Word of God and an entirely different thing to honor what it says. The Bible is divine instruction for you to live by. God's desire is that you abide in him and his Word to abide in you. Fulfill his desire and he will fulfill yours.

# Day 29

## God's Word

Read God's Word with the intention of following and obeying. As you surrender every area of your life, obedience to the written Word of God becomes effortless. The more intimate your relationship with your Bridegroom, the more you will desire to follow his commands and decrees. Start sowing seeds of obedience into the future you're praying and seeking.

## Key Verse

"Jesus replied, 'But even more blessed are all who hear the Word of God and put it into practice.'" (Luke 11:28 NLT)

## Prayer Key

❁Help me apply your Word to my life

❁I want to be obedient to your Word

❁Help me follow your commands and decrees

❁I want to sow seeds of obedience into my future

God spoke to my heart …

My thoughts …

# Day 30

## Fruits of the Spirit

Your intimacy with the Lord gives way to spiritual growth. This growth manifests itself through the blossoming of spiritual fruit. As you give the Holy Spirit room in your life to expand and increase, the more manifestation of fruit. Everything the world drains you of is replenished and abundantly supplied through the Spirit of God. Stay on track. Your intimacy with God leads to a beautiful everlasting spiritual garden.

## Key Verse

"But the fruit of the Spirit [the result of His presence within us] is love [unselfish concern for others], joy, [inner] peace, patience [not the ability to wait, but how we act while waiting], kindness, goodness, faithfulness, gentleness, self-control." (Galatians 5:22-23 AMP)

## Prayer Key

❃Holy Spirit increase in me

❃Help me decrease

❃I desire spiritual growth

❃May the fruits of the Spirit manifest

God spoke to my heart …

My thoughts …

# Day 31

## God's Truths

***God is infallible. God's love never fails. God's power is unlimited. God's character never changes. God forgives.***

It's necessary to know God's truths because they directly counteract the lies of the enemy. God's truths are your antidote for the viral lies the world believes. Lies that will try to poison your walk with Christ. God's truths have been tested throughout time and they never fail. As you travel through dark stretches of life, you will learn to depend on these truths for strength and peace of mind.

## Key Verse

"And you will know the truth, and the truth will set you free."
(John 8:32 NLT)

## Prayer Key

❁May your truths become my truths

❁Help me depend on your truths

❁Tune out the lies

❁May your truths give me strength and peace of mind

God spoke to my heart …

My thoughts …

# Day 32

## God's Promises

The heavenly Bridegroom that you anxiously await is coming for you. That's not a fairytale. That's a PROMISE! God's promises are for you to take as your own and apply them to your life. His divine promises infuse hope and give a supernatural perspective. They give you a glimpse of things to come and fuel your faith. Read the Word and seek his beautiful promises written for the enrichment of your life—promises written ***once upon a time*** with your future in mind.

## Key Verse

"So My Word which goes from My mouth will not return to Me empty. It will do what I want it to do, and will carry out My plan well." (Isaiah 55:11 NLT)

## Prayer Key

❁Highlight your promises

❁Help me apply them to my life

❁Help me believe them

❁Fuel my faith

God spoke to my heart ...

My thoughts ...

# Day 33

## God's Presence

God says, "Seek me and you will find me." God's presence is essential to your spiritual growth. Seek him with the intention of encountering him, because it's through God's presence that hidden things become revealed. Encountering the Lord's supremacy straightens things out in your life you didn't know were crooked. Things that seem right are shown for what they truly are under his Holy light.

## Key Verse

"You will seek me and find me when you seek me with all your heart." (Jeremiah 29:13 NIV)

## Prayer Key

- ❁Lord, I want to encounter you
- ❁Reveal hidden things
- ❁Bring order to my life
- ❁Open my spiritual eyes

God spoke to my heart ...

My thoughts ...

# Day 34

## HOLY SPIRIT

You are but a jar of clay with a beautiful treasure inside called the Holy Spirit. Give the Spirit liberty to do what's necessary to prepare you for your next season. Yield to the Spirit and he will purge things that have hindered your growth in the past. Allow him to use this waiting period to mold you into something beautiful that can be used in the future for his glory and to further his kingdom.

## KEY VERSE

"He must increase, but I must decrease." (John 3:30 ESV)

## PRAYER KEY

❁Help my flesh decrease as you increase

❁I yield to your Spirit

❁Do the necessary work in me

❁Use this season for your glory

God spoke to my heart ...

My thoughts ...

# Day 35

## God's Principles

Your Heavenly Father is a good Father, and as such he teaches, rebukes, corrects, and builds up through Scripture. God's principles are like a guidebook, designed to shepherd you through life righteously, not a set of rules or dos and don'ts. God the Father loves you; therefore, his principles are for the edification and enrichment of your life. Living by his principles will safeguard you from destructive decisions and patterns.

## Key Verse

"Where there is no guidance, a people falls, but in an abundance of counselors there is safety." (Proverbs 11:14 ESV)

## Prayer Key

❁I want to live by your biblical principles

❁Help me live righteously

❁Edify and enrich my life

❁Guide me through life

God spoke to my heart …

My thoughts …

# Week Six

## A Servant's Heart

Activate your heart to serve the Lord and his purpose. As you pray, God's gifts, which have remained dormant inside of you, begin to awaken and function. The next seven days are filled with heavenly discoveries which will bless you, but more importantly bless others as well as build God's kingdom.

# Day 36

## Unwrapping My Gifts

God created you with supernatural gifts waiting to be discovered. Once these gifts are revealed, they need to be unwrapped and developed. This comes as you seek intimacy and spiritual maturity in the Lord. There are many gifts; seeking revelation brings clarity and direction towards the uncovering of your spiritual gifts. Jesus is expectantly waiting for you to take this important step so he can use you effectively in furthering his kingdom.

## Key Verse

"For this reason I remind you to fan into flame the gift of God." (2 Timothy 1:6 NIV)

## Prayer Key

❀Reveal my gift

❀Give me clarity and direction

❀Develop my gift

❀May my gift be used for your glory

God spoke to my heart …

My thoughts …

# Day 37

## Use My Talents

You are born with talents to edify and bless the body of Christ. These unique abilities are given to you by God and intended for his glory. Using your talents for the Lord brings forth blessing not only for others but also for you. Your talents set you apart and add layers to your purpose. God entrusted you with talents, gifts, and abilities—use them wisely.

## Key Verse

"Just as each one of you has received a special gift [a spiritual talent, an ability graciously given by God], employ it in serving one another as [is appropriate for] good stewards of God's multi-faceted grace [faithfully using the diverse, varied gifts and abilities granted to Christians by God's unmerited favor]." (1 Peter 4:10 AMP)

## Prayer Key

- ❁Use my talents
- ❁May my talents bring you glory
- ❁Help me use my talents to bless others

God spoke to my heart ...

My thoughts ...

# Day 38

## Hearing God's Call

Understanding God's call on your life requires that you hear his voice. His voice may be discerned through his Word. He may also speak into your heart through the Holy Spirit. The closer your walk with Christ the louder and more defined his voice becomes. The more intimately you know the Shepherd the easier it becomes to differentiate his voice from others. Once you hear his call… obey it. He will lead you towards your purpose and align your present with the future in which you are praying.

## Key Verse

"The sheep that are My own hear My voice and listen to Me; I know them, and they follow Me." (John 10:27 AMP)

## Prayer Key

- ❅Make me sensitive to your voice
- ❅Tune out destructive voices
- ❅Help me obey your call
- ❅Align my present with my future

God spoke to my heart ...

My thoughts ...

# Day 39

## Fulfilling My Purpose

Many people live and then die without discovering their purpose for life. From birth, your Father God assigned to your life a purpose—a divine purpose only he's able to reveal. Seek him with all your heart and he will show you things you never knew and breathe life into your season. It will renew your strength with vision of the future and the role you play in fulfillment. Purpose gives perspective. Perspective births peace. Peace will nurture contentment into your season as you expectantly wait on the Lord.

## Key Verse

"But I have raised you up for this very purpose, that I might show you my power and that my name might be proclaimed in all the earth." (Exodus 9:16 NIV)

## Prayer Key

- ❁What is my purpose
- ❁Grant me vision of the future and my role in its fulfillment
- ❁May my purpose give way to perspective, peace, and contentment

God spoke to my heart …

My thoughts …

# Day 40

## Activating My Faith

God is using each season to further his intentions in your life. His purpose is to draw you closer to him and create an unshakable faith that will bless and enhance your next season. Every emotion you experience—loneliness, sadness, or isolation—God desires to use as a trigger to activate your faith. He doesn't want you to dwell or complacently stay in that feeling, but use it as a catapult to mobilize your faith in Christ.

## Key Verse

"In the same way, faith by itself, if it is not accompanied by action, is dead." (James 2:17 NIV)

## Prayer Key

❁Use this season for your glory, Lord

❁May I use the triggers to activate my faith

❁Activate my faith

❁I don't want to dwell but be catapulted

God spoke to my heart …

My thoughts …

# Day 41

## The Heart of Worship

Throughout the Word of God, the heart of worship is evident. Mary, Anna the Prophetess, and Lydia—these women were known as worshippers because they chose worship above all other things. Their sole focus was Jesus Christ and their worship pleased and moved the Lord. Your worship will too! Commit to choose worship over worrying or complaining and watch as the showers of blessings fall upon your barren season and produce a harvest.

## Key Verse

"But the hour is coming, and is not here, when the true worshipers will worship the Father in spirit and truth, for the Father is seeking such people to worship him. God is spirit, and those who worship him must worship in spirit and truth." (John 4:23-24 ESV)

## Prayer Key

- ❁Give me a heart of worship
- ❁Help me choose worship
- ❁May my worship be honest and transparent
- ❁Focus on Jesus

God spoke to my heart ...

My thoughts ...

# Day 42

## Humble and Ready

Pride obstructs God's work by hardening your heart and destroys what God has created. Often pride resides hidden in the heart without notice until God draws you to obedience. God opposes the proud but gives grace to the humble. Your desire is to be in harmony with the Lord, working together through your journey. Having a humble heart and attitude allows God to initiate change and align you with his purpose.

## Key Verse

"Before his downfall a man's heart is proud, but humility comes before honor." (Proverbs 18:12 HCSB)

## Prayer Key

- ❁Remove all pride, Lord
- ❁Give me a humble heart
- ❁Harmony with Jesus
- ❁Initiate change and align me

God spoke to my heart ...

My thoughts ...

# Week Seven

## Seeking Holiness

Praying "hard prayers" requires intentionality and an honest heart. Do not be apprehensive as you approach each new day. On the contrary, praise and banish all fear in the name of Jesus. Seeking holiness will reap a harvest unlike anything you've ever seen before.

# Day 43

## Wash Me Clean

To be an effective tool for the Lord you must seek holiness. It's not just about believing in Jesus. It's about deliberately following his lead and being holy like Jesus. The fallen world around you is vying for your heart every day. Everything you watch, read, or hear seeks to taint your thoughts and ultimately influence your choices. Pursue holiness through prayer and the Lord will honor your request by revealing sin through his loving conviction.

## Key Verse

"For it is written: 'Be holy, because I am holy." (1 Peter 1:16 NIV)

## Prayer Key

- ❁Holy Spirit conviction
- ❁Help me pursue holiness
- ❁Reveal the sin in my life

God spoke to my heart ...

My thoughts ...

# Day 44

## Search Me

God is aware of everything. He hears your thoughts and knows the intentions of your heart and yet he longs to hear you say, "Search me, God." Why? Because it's evidence you're yearning for righteousness. This is a bold and powerful prayer in which you yield and grant the Lord full access to search and prune everything he deems fruitless, and then breathes new life into your journey.

## Key Verse

"Search me, God, and know my heart; test me and know my anxious thoughts. See if there is any offensive way in me, and lead me in the way everlasting!" (Psalm 139:23-24 NIV)

## Prayer Key

- ❁Search me, God
- ❁Reveal and remove anything fruitless in my life
- ❁Breathe new life

God spoke to my heart …

My thoughts …

# Day 45

## Use Me

Be intentional and make yourself available for Jesus to use you as a chosen vessel. He knows you better than you know yourself; therefore, only he knows how best to utilize your gifts, talents, and strengths. What you have in mind for your life might not be God's best for your unique qualifications. So far you have played it safe and stayed in your comfort zone, but God's ways are higher than yours. He will stretch your faith by leading you to serve in ways you never thought possible.

## Key Verse

"Therefore, if anyone cleanses himself from what is dishonorable, he will be a vessel for honorable use, set apart as holy, useful to the master of the house, ready for every good work." (2 Timothy 2:21 ESV)

## Prayer Key

❁Use me, Lord

❁Stretch me

❁Lead me

❁Give me strength to obey your call

God spoke to my heart ...

My thoughts ...

# Day 46

## CHANGE ME

When you encountered Jesus and accepted his salvation you were made new. You were sealed by the Holy Spirit and therefore empowered to make changes in your life that are only possible with God's help. Since day one, the Holy Spirit has been transforming you, but you must grant him permission into areas that have been off limits in the past. Secret compartments in your heart which may be fostering lust or unforgiveness must be unlocked for the Holy Spirit to commence the change you seek.

## KEY VERSE

"Create in me a clean heart, O God, and renew a right spirit within me." (Psalm 51:10 ESV)

## PRAYER KEY

❁Change me

❁I give you full access into my heart

❁Do away with anything that does not honor you

❁Break strongholds

God spoke to my heart ...

My thoughts ...

# Day 47

## I Submit

Joyfully submit to the process, without fear or doubt, because God is a good God. Confidently yield and do not resist when the Holy Spirit prompts you to change the way you deal with anger or to let go of someone who has no place in your future. These changes are often uncomfortable and some painful, but the spiritual growth you will gain will be worth it.

## Key Verse

"Teach me to do your will, for you are my God; may your good Spirit lead me on level ground." (Psalm 143:10 NIV)

## Prayer Key

❁Give me joy in the midst

❁I welcome change

❁Give me strength

❁Help me do your will

God spoke to my heart …

My thoughts …

# Day 48

## Have Your Way, Lord

These past few days you have offered up bold prayers. They are effective and are certain to gain God's attention, rendering a quick response. These hard (difficult) prayers obtain priority status because they shake the earth. Your desire to honor God pleases him and moves his heart because these requests deal with eternal things. When you seek to honor him with the eternal, by nature, he will supply the temporal.

## Key Verse

"Your Kingdom come, your will be done, on earth as it is in heaven." (Matthew 6:10 NIV)

## Prayer Key

❁My desire is to honor you

❁Give me a kingdom mind

❁Have your way in me

❁Keep me focused on the eternal

God spoke to my heart ...

My thoughts ...

# Day 49

## Wisdom and Understanding

Change does not come easy. It's a process of renewing old mindsets and deleting old patterns. God's wisdom will help you conform to the new he is doing in your life. Understanding will help you discern what you need to let go and not pursue. It will also guide you down the path of least resistance which is in obedience to God's will and purpose in your life.

## Key Verse

"Do not turn away from her (Wisdom) and she will guard and protect you; the beginning of wisdom is: Get [skillful and godly] wisdom [it is preeminent]! And with all your acquiring, get understanding [actively seek spiritual discernment, mature comprehension, and logical interpretation]." (Proverbs 4:6-7 AMP)

## Prayer Key

❀Give me wisdom

❀Help me gain understanding

❀Give me a discerning heart

❀May I obey and honor you with my life

God spoke to my heart …

My thoughts …

# Week Eight

## My Everyday Life

In your daily life the mundane is of utmost importance to the Lord, because you are His. God wants to be front and center in your life with nothing off limits. Placing God at the core of your life will release peace and contentment into everything else.

# Day 50

## My Family

Your relationships have an impact on your spiritual life, especially relationships with family, so it's important to cover them with prayer. God didn't accidentally place people in your life; there is intention behind each connection, whether blood related or not. Many times, God uses these imperfect, complex relationships to refine your character, which is often painful at first but a blessing in the end.

## Key Verse

"How good and pleasant it is when God's people live together in unity!" (Psalm 133:1 NIV)

## Prayer Key

❁Thank you for my family

❁Bless them

❁Give me grace towards them

❁Give us unity

God spoke to my heart …

My thoughts …

# Day 51

## My Friends

Friends are a blessing when chosen wisely. Through the book of Proverbs God warns us of associating with bad company and the consequences of poor judgement. As you continue seeking the kingdom of God, he will give you everything you need...that includes friends! During your single journey it is essential to surround yourself with a tribe of strong women of God. A loyal squad who will not only encourage you but pray and stand in the gap for you.

## Key Verse

"As iron sharpens iron, so a friend sharpens a friend." (Proverbs 27:17 NLT)

## Prayer Key

❁Bless my friends

❁Guide me to choose wisely

❁Send me a tribe of godly women

❁Help me be a loyal friend

God spoke to my heart …

My thoughts …

# Day 52

## My Occupation

Your life's occupation is important to the Lord. Whether you attend school or work full time, he wants to be a part of your world. In all you do, God encourages a godly work ethic, one with integrity and passion. His leading will inspire you to venture out and try new things. His favor will open doors that defy human logic. His protection will close doors that lead to dead ends. And his wisdom will help you surpass any human knowledge.

## Key Verse

"Whatever you do, work at it with all your heart, as working for the Lord, not for human masters, since you know that you will receive an inheritance from the Lord as a reward. It is the Lord Christ you are serving." (Colossians 3:23-24 NIV)

## Prayer Key

❁I invite you into my everyday life

❁May I always exemplify a godly work ethic

❁Lead me to new opportunities

❁Favor, protect, and give me wisdom

God spoke to my heart …

My thoughts …

# Day 53

## My Home

Your home is a reflection of you. As your prayer life increases and your relationship with Jesus deepens, your life will begin to radiate the changes that have taken place. The peace that has settled in your heart will quickly make its way into your home and create a tranquil environment for anyone who enters in turmoil. Your newfound joy will resonate through the air and revitalize those with a heavy heart. Friends and visitors will be blessed as they encounter the presence of Jesus just by walking through your front door.

## Key Verse

"By wisdom a house is built, and by understanding it is established; by knowledge the rooms are filled with all precious and pleasant riches." (Proverbs 24:3-4 ESV)

## Prayer Key

❁Fill my home

❁Bless those who walk through the door

❁May my home glorify you, Lord

❁I want my home to radiate your goodness

God spoke to my heart …

My thoughts …

# Day 54

## My Time

Each day is a gift from God, so your time is valuable. Learn to be efficient with your time by creating and keeping an agenda or a planner. Make time for projects the Lord has secretly placed in your heart but somehow never started. Set goals for yourself (e.g., ministry or writing a book) and schedule time each day to work on them. Having a scheduled course of action will help you stay on track and lead you to accomplish things you put off for lack of time.

## Key Verse

"For everything there is an appointed time, and an appropriate time for every activity on earth:" (Ecclesiastes 3:1 NET Bible)

## Prayer Key

❁Help me manage my time

❁I want to prioritize the things you placed in my heart

❁Align my goals with you

❁Help me accomplish what I start

God spoke to my heart ...

My thoughts ...

# Day 55

## My Finances

Honor the Lord with your money and he will provide abundantly for all your needs. Create a budget which includes a specified amount labeled "God money." Carry it with you and when led by the Spirit, give it to someone in need. Be creative and use your money for the glory of God. Your Father calls you to be a good steward, so spend wisely, avoid borrowing and save up for the future you are praying for and desiring.

## Key Verse

"Each of you should give what you have decided in your heart to give, not reluctantly or under compulsion, for God loves a cheerful giver. And God is able to bless you abundantly, so that in all things at all times, having all that you need, you will abound in every good work." (2 Corinthians 9:7-8 NIV)

## Prayer Key

❁Lord, I want to honor you with my finances

❁Remind me to always carry "God money"

❁Holy Spirit lead me to people in need

❁Help me be a good steward

God spoke to my heart …

My thoughts …

# Day 56

## My Health

Your body is the temple of the Holy Spirit. God values your body. What you eat and how you treat your body is important to God because it houses his Spirit. Be mindful and eat nutritious foods that will edify and nurture your body. Exercise frequently and pray to ward off unnecessary diseases that will only hamper your ability to serve the Lord effectively. Make sure to get plenty of sleep and allow your body to heal, repair, and restore itself. Be disciplined and honor and glorify God with your body.

## Key Verse

"Do you not know that your bodies are temples of the Holy Spirit, who is in you, whom you have received from God? You are not your own; you were bought at a price. Therefore honor God with your bodies." (1 Corinthians 6:20 NIV)

## Prayer Key

- ❈Help me make wise choices when I eat
- ❈Give me the energy to exercise
- ❈I want to be disciplined
- ❈May I honor and glorify you with my body

God spoke to my heart ...

My thoughts ...

# Week Nine

## Order My Steps

Your time matters to God. As you continue to surrender your will, God brings structure and peace to your days. The Holy Spirit alerts you to things breeding stress in your life that need to change. You will be surprised as the Lord starts arranging priorities in your life you once believed were perfect.

# Day 57

## Organize My Life

God is a God of peace, not chaos. An unorganized life breeds stress and disorder. A dysfunctional relationship, a job that leaves no time for Jesus, constantly changing majors, or being a serial dater are a few examples of things that lead to a disorderly life. Allow God to rearrange and purge the things causing the chaos and therefore bring order, so his peace may dwell in your life.

## Key Verse

"For God is not a God of disorder but of peace." (1 Corinthians 14:33 NIV)

## Prayer Key

- ❁Organize my life
- ❁Rearrange and purge whatever does not belong
- ❁Bring order to my relationships, school, work etc.
- ❁I desire your peace

God spoke to my heart ...

My thoughts ...

# Day 58

## Better Decisions

Unfortunately, many of our decisions are emotionally driven, especially those dealing with relationships. It's important you seek God when making decisions because he knows past your lifeline and is aware of how it all turns out. Remember, the decisions you make today will shape your life. God's divine intervention will ensure your present and future remain aligned with his will.

## Key Verse

"I will instruct you and teach you in the way you should go; I will counsel you with my loving eye on you." (Psalm 32:8 NIV)

## Prayer Key

❁Help me make better decisions

❁Align my choices with your will

❁Instruct and teach me, Lord

❁Lead me to your best

God spoke to my heart …

My thoughts …

# Day 59

## Pleasing God Not Man

People pleasing is a trap that will ensnare and make you a slave to other people. God urges us to care and love one another but not necessarily become a servant. It's impossible to please everyone. And yet, the enemy uses the desire to please others to weigh you down and weaken you, physically and emotionally. Christ desires to deliver you from the stronghold of people pleasing so you may develop and nurture healthy relationships with others.

## Key Verse

"I'm not trying to win the approval of people, but of God. If pleasing people were my goal, I would not be Christ's servant." (Galatians 1:10 NLT)

## Prayer Key

- ❀Deliver me from people pleasing
- ❀I only want to please you, Lord
- ❀May I seek first the kingdom of God
- ❀Reveal anything or anyone that has taken your place in my life

God spoke to my heart …

My thoughts …

# Day 60

## YES, LORD!

In this journey God is doing a new thing in your life. For the new to be activated you must listen and obey his leading. How many times have you felt the urge to help someone in need or felt the tug to witness to a stranger, but out of fear you have ignored the Holy Spirit? It's time to change the automatic response and start saying, "YES, Lord." For years the safe zone has been your home, but God is encouraging you to step out in faith and say YES to his calling. The more you say YES, the more comfortable you become as he stretches your comfort zones.

## KEY VERSE

"Surrender your whole being to him to be used for righteous purposes." (Romans 6:13b GNT)

## PRAYER KEY

❁I want to say, Yes, Lord.

❁Attach an urgency to your call

❁Remove all fear so I may obey

❁Help me discern your voice

God spoke to my heart …

My thoughts …

# Day 61

## New Things

God is doing a new thing inside of you, do you perceive it? As you walk into the new, the old will no longer feel or fit the same. This is a great season to try new things! Through this journey the Lord has been aligning your heart to his, so trust the Holy Spirit's leading. Take that new job offer. Change majors. Take the trip you're putting off. Move to the city the Lord continues to impress upon your heart. God's new will rarely look like what you expect. He will always exceed your expectations.

## Key Verse

"Now unto him that is able to do exceedingly abundantly above all that we ask or think, according to the power that worketh in us." (Ephesians 3:20 KJV)

## Prayer Key

❁Help me welcome the new

❁Make me fearless and courageous

❁Lead me to walk in the new

❁Give me discernment as I try new things

God spoke to my heart ...

My thoughts ...

# Day 62

## Quiet My Fears

Your life is taking a turn for good. The Lord is blessing and favoring your path as you seek his presence daily. You're at peace and content as you wait on God. But do not let your guard down. Be alert, because the father of lies will try to halt your momentum and destroy what you have gained in the Lord by instilling fear into your mind and heart. Be steadfast in Christ and put on the full armor of God every morning so you can stand against the devil's schemes and overcome.

## Key Verse

"The thief comes only to steal and kill and destroy. I came that they may have life and have it abundantly." (John 10:10 ESV)

## Prayer Key

- Lord, quiet my fears
- Shield me from the devil's schemes
- May I believe your truths over the lies
- Help me discern the lies

God spoke to my heart ...

My thoughts ...

# Day 63

## Make Me Bold

You've been nurturing your spiritual roots as they've grown deeper into the Lord. Your faith is stronger, and your identity rooted through every prayer you've made. You are now ready and equipped. Be bold and outspoken about Christ and your faith. Remember, the mouth speaks of what the heart is full." (Luke 6:45) At this point in time your heart should be overflowing and ready to pour into someone else.

## Key Verse

"And he said to them, 'Go into all the world and proclaim the gospel to the whole creation.'" (Mark 16:15 ESV)

## Prayer Key

- ❁Give me an urgency to spread the gospel
- ❁Make me bold and unashamed
- ❁Guide me to people who need to be poured into
- ❁Help me speak and share your truths

God spoke to my heart ...

My thoughts ...

# Week Ten

## My Future

As you pray over your future, concentrate on things to come. God will fill you with expectant hope and joy. Get ready as God positions you for his blessings. Pray, then prepare for what you've asked. Pray and believe that God's plans will be fulfilled in your life. He loves you.

# Day 64

## My Future

You've let go of the past and you've aligned your present with the Lord. Now you must pray in preparation of your future. God knows what your future holds because he planned and designed it that way. He is the author of your life, your story. Surrender any apprehensions or fears of the unknown and trust that whatever is to come will be for your good and to ultimately fulfill God's purpose in your life.

## Key Verse

"'For I know the plans I have for you,' declares the LORD, 'plans to prosper you and not to harm you, plans to give you hope and a future.'" (Jeremiah 29:11 NIV)

## Prayer Key

- I surrender my fears over an unknown future
- Prepare me for what's to come
- My plans are in your hands
- Thank you because you have divine plans for my life

God spoke to my heart ...

My thoughts ...

# Day 65

## A Godly Wife

In the Christian dating realm, you often hear, "pray for a godly husband," because it's important. But even more so, it's important to pray to be worthy of such a man. This prayer journey laid the groundwork for God to transform you into a godly wife. Remember, everything Ruth went through was in preparation of her Boaz. Was she a perfect woman? Absolutely not, but her submission moved God to rewrite her story, a story which until this day inspires hope to Christian single women around the world.

## Key Verse

"A wife of noble character who can find? She is worth far more than rubies." (Proverbs 31:10)

## Prayer Key

❁May I be worthy of a godly husband

❁Help me become a godly wife

❁Prepare me for my Boaz

❁Teach me, lead me, and guide me

God spoke to my heart ...

My thoughts ...

# Day 66

## My Future Husband

Your husband already exists and is currently walking the face of this earth, so it's important to cover him in prayer. He is also in preparation and facing trials and temptations just like you. Intercede for him in faith and be an active part of his life. You've never seen him, but God knows him, long before in his mother's womb. How beautiful the moment when you say to him, "I prayed for you even before I met you."

## Key Verse

"Blessed is she who has believed that the Lord would fulfill his promises to her!" (Luke 1:45 NIV)

## Prayer Key

- ❁Bless him, Lord
- ❁Protect him
- ❁Lead him
- ❁Prepare him for our life together

God spoke to my heart …

My thoughts …

# Day 67

## My Future In-laws

Your future in-laws will play a big part in your married life. Praying for them is important because the process of integrating into a new family is often stressful and difficult. As you pray, God will go before you, preparing hearts and minds for a smooth transition. He will highly favor you in their eyes and bless the relationship.

## Key Verse

"With all humility and gentleness, with patience, bearing with one another in love, eager to maintain the unity of the Spirit in the bond of peace." (Ephesians 4:2-3 ESV)

## Prayer Key

❋May we love and accept each other

❋May it be a blessed relationship

❋Give us unity of mind

❋May we be grateful for our new family

God spoke to my heart ...

My thoughts ...

# Day 68

## Prepare My Heart for Marriage

Marriage is more than the wedding day and the honeymoon. Marriage is beautiful but difficult work. It requires communication, compromise, forgiveness, compassion, and so much more to achieve a successful lifelong union. Asking God to prepare your heart for marriage will help you overcome situations that perhaps would be detrimental to your young marriage.

## Key Verse

"Love is patient and kind; love does not envy or boast, it is not arrogant or rude. It does not insist on its own way; it is not irritable or resentful; it does not rejoice at wrongdoing, but rejoices with the truth. Love bears all things, believes all things, hopes all things, endures all things. Love never ends." (1 Corinthians 13:4-8 NIV)

## Prayer Key

- ❀Prepare my heart for marriage
- ❀Help my heart bear all things, believe all things, hope all things, and endure all things
- ❀Prepare my heart to overcome future situations peacefully and in love
- ❀Prepare my heart to love unconditionally

God spoke to my heart …

My thoughts …

# Day 69

## Prepare My Mind for Marriage

We have many preconceived notions of marriage that need to be abolished before entering this holy covenant. When you think of marriage you have certain expectations, but what if your expectations never match your experience? There is nothing wrong with dreaming of a fairytale wedding, but it's essential to prepare for the real-life aspects of married life.

## Key Verse

"What therefore God hath joined together, let not man put asunder." (Mark 10:9 KJV)

## Prayer Key

- ❁Prepare my mind to be one flesh
- ❁Remove any preconceived notions that don't align with a godly marriage
- ❁Abolish unrealistic expectations
- ❁Prepare my mind for the real-life aspects of marriage

God spoke to my heart ...

My thoughts ...

# Day 70

## MARRIAGE?

From an early age, girls are led to believe a knight in shining armor will one day arrive to rescue them. Thank God, for Christian women, that knight has already arrived. His name is Jesus Christ, and he supernaturally completes the heart in a way no human ever will. Many of those impressionable girls will grow up and marry, but the reality is that some will not. For some, marriage is simply not part of their story and that's okay. Through the years I've spoken to many women whom have remained single, and the one thing they all have in common is the peace God has given them over their singleness.

## KEY VERSE

"For your Maker is your husband, the Lord Almighty is his name, the Holy One of Israel is your Redeemer; he is called the God of all the earth." (Isaiah 54:5 NIV)

## PRAYER KEY

❀Give me peace over my singleness

❀Help me be content

❀Fill my life and heart with joy

❀Give me dreams for a fruitful future

God spoke to my heart ...

My thoughts ...

# Conclusion

You've reached the end of this journal; however, your journey continues. You are on a course which requires deliberateness. You've made significant progress, but you must stay on track to maintain momentum and keep from reverting back to old patterns. Keep praying and seeking the Lord purposefully. Resist the temptation to slack in your pursuit of righteousness and press on. Revisit your *Praying Through Singleness* journal as many times as needed and re-read the days that perhaps were challenging. There are topics that require intense prayer. Praying again over areas of struggle is encouraged.

*Don't stop journaling!* Use an ordinary notebook or go all out and buy an adorable journal. It does not matter. What is important is making a habit of journaling through your season. I've been journaling for years and one of my favorite things to read is my old ledgers. Page after page, God's fingerprints start appearing as if fingerprint powder has been dusted throughout. As you read your old entries, God's presence becomes evident and his work visible. Your journals will bear witness to God's faithfulness in your life. Your own written words will proclaim, "God did it once. He will do it again."

*Continue reading the Word of God.* Look up the Bible verses you've read these past ten weeks and go deeper—read the whole chapter. Challenge yourself and memorize the Bible verses as you meditate on them. I reiterate this throughout the journal because it's of the utmost importance to stay strong and steadfast. God's Word is active and gives life; it reveals truth and shatters lies. The Lord blesses those who read the Word of God and obey it.

*Put your prayers into action.* You've prayed. Now mobilize and ready yourself for God's use. Don't be surprised if God places you in situations that will activate what he's placed inside of you. He may want you to share your experience and purposefully position people around you that need what you've gained in this season. Don't shy away from these or similar scenarios out of fear. Exercising your spiritual gifts will further develop them for the kingdom of God.

Singlehood is a beautiful season of preparation. Don't let the world dictate your timeline; concentrate on being present. Fix your eyes on him and he will light the path before you. Don't worry yourself with what's to come or the unknown. El Roi (the God who sees) SEES you. He sees and hears your worries because you are precious to him. Let go and relax. Enjoy this time of singleness and do not hold back. Smile and be joyful! A frail, lonely, single girl drives others away, but a woman who radiates confidence and knows who she is in Christ attracts positive attention. Your life can be a testimony for the glory of God. Don't waste this moment in time, wishing it away, instead take advantage of your freedom in Christ.

Be positive and your outlook will follow. Speak words that edify your life. Build up and refuse to tear down that which God deems worthy. Yes, you are worthy. God paid a high price for you, so don't be enslaved by thoughts that are not uplifting. The Lord has given you the authority to take negative thoughts captive. You're a strong godly woman—exert that power.

The enemy will try to destroy your progress by distracting you through the opinions of others. But remember, when you're secure in Christ, you no longer require anyone's approval because you're validated. Rejection becomes redirection. A hookup is replaced by a heavenly setup. Your waiting turns into preparation. You're unstoppable because you KNOW who you are and WHOSE you are. Now go and share this wisdom! You are the light that will shine hope to many hopeless and lost singles. Don't keep this treasure hidden, share your hope in Christ!

# About Shayla

Shayla Ortiz created My Single Purpose in 2011. Her passion for serving Christ led her to discover a unique way to serve the Lord without ever stepping foot outside her home, through social media. Eights years later her mission remains unchanged, and that is to reach young singles, meet them right where they are for the sole purpose of breathing life and hope into their lives.

Shayla resides in Georgia with her loving husband and three pretty cool teenagers. When she's not busy writing or encouraging, she enjoys long walks, horseback riding trails, and learning other languages.


Connect with Shayla at:

MySinglePurpose.com

Facebook.com/mysinglepurpose

Facebook.com/Shaylablessed

Instagram: @mysinglepurpose

Mysinglepurpose.tumblr.com

YouTube.com/mysinglepurpose

Made in the USA
Middletown, DE
15 July 2019